WORKERS' COMPENSATION 101

Andre' Ramsay, Esq.

WORKERS' COMPENSATION

101

Workers' Compensation Do's and Don'ts for Injured Workers in Georgia

Andre' Ramsay, Esq.

Contents

Introduction

If you, a family member, friend or loved one has been injured on the job, this guide is for you. This guide is a compilation of dozens of videos, podcasts and frequently asked questions condensed into an easy to read format. Links to the videos have also been included. This guide will also answer the following frequently asked questions:

What is workers' compensation?

Am I eligible for benefits under workers' compensation?

How long do I have to work to be covered?

When do I have to report an injury?

Do I have to see a doctor?

What if it is an emergency?

Why can't I use my doctor?

What if I need a specialist?

Who pays for the medical care?

What is covered?

How long can I get benefits?

What is a catastrophic injury?

When do my benefits start?

How much will I get?

How long can I get benefits?

What if my injury keeps me from getting a job?

What benefits will I get if my injury causes permanent disability?

What if I lose an arm, a leg or some other body part?

What if I am blinded or made deaf?

What if I lose the ability to use part of my body?

What are death benefits?

Can I get Workers' Compensation and Social Security at the same time?

What if I am not getting my workers' compensation benefits?

How do I file a claim?

What happens when I file a claim?

Do I need a lawyer?

How much will a lawyer cost me?

It is our hope that this guide will help educate injured workers' about their rights, and answer questions about workers' compensation. If you are facing a legal issue and need help, please contact me directly at aramsay@cochranfirmatl.com or call our firm directly at 404-222-9922. There is no fee or obligation for the first consultation.

Workers' Compensation Attorney: Do's and Don'ts for Injured Workers

https://www.youtube.com/watch?v=4M-wIdHgQRc

Interviewer:

Thank you so much for joining our event today; Workers' Compensation 101, and Workers' Compensation Do's and Don'ts for Injured Workers. It is being presented by Atty. Andre' Ramsay who's with The Cochran Firm Atlanta. Atty. Andre' C. Ramsay joined The Cochran Firm Atlanta in 2016.

Mr. Ramsay previously worked as an associate attorney at a fast-paced north Atlanta law firm specializing in the practice areas of workers' compensation, personal injury, and social security disability. Mr. Ramsay aggressively represents many injured workers in acquiring all income and medical benefits available to them to the full extent of the law.

Mr. Ramsay earned a Bachelor's degree in Management of Information Studies with a minor in Business Administration from Florida State University. As an undergraduate student, Andre' was one of sixteen students chosen from twenty three states for the Florida State University College of Law National Summer Law Program. Mr. Ramsay later earned his Juris Doctor degree from Atlanta's John Marshall Law School. While in law school, Andre' completed the American Bar Association Client Interviewing and Counseling competition where he placed in the national top six after winning the regional competition. Andre' also found that the Caribbean Law Students Association, a student bar association class representative, and Pre-trial Calley Award recipient. Andre' also clerked for a well known National law firm, where he had the opportunity to work directly under a form of Georgia workers' compensation administrative law judge.

Mr. Ramsay, are you there?

Mr. Ramsay:

I am. I'm so happy to be here to try to provide some good advice to people who need it.

Interviewer:

We are happy to have you. Now, if you're on the call, listening to the event or reading our book, or if you've ever wondered what benefits injured workers are entitled to receive, you're going to receive some great advice today -

What do you do if you have a preexisting injury?

What happens after receiving medical care for an injury?

What happens if you wait to report an injury?

You're going to have these questions answered and more. So, Mr. Ramsay I'm going to ask you a few questions and we're going to walk through all of the information for our listeners and readers today.

What Benefits Are Injured Workers Entitled to Receive? Georgia Workers' Compensation

https://www.youtube.com/watch?v=JrFlrI_EtX4

What benefits are injured workers entitled to receive?

Mr. Ramsay:

They're entitled to receive three core benefits. The first of which would be income benefits. Income benefits are split out into three types of income benefits so stay with me. The first type of benefit, that's an income benefit - it's called Temporary Total Disability. The injured worker receives those benefits if they're taken out of work due to their injury or if they're placed on light duty restrictions from their doctor, and their employer is unwilling to or cannot provide or accommodate the light duty restriction that's given to them by their doctor.

Now, this income benefit - Temporary Total Disability (TTD) - is typically two thirds of what the person makes on an average week. It's not going to be a dollar for dollar amount that you've lost from the income due to the injury. For instance, if you earn $500 per week - unfortunately you'll receive between $325-$360 or so per week. So that's something that the injured worker needs to be aware of - because your bills certainly don't get minimized by two thirds but your income does. That's the first income benefit that they receive.

The second income benefit that you can receive is called Temporary Partial Disability or TPD benefits. That benefit is if you're placed on light duty and your employer can accommodate you, and you're working a light duty position. If you're earning less money than you did before the injury, then the employer owes you two thirds of the difference between the two. So for instance, you're earning again $500 per week, and now you're working a light duty position that affords you $400 per week, the employer owes you two thirds of that $100 difference or $66 per week.

The third type of income benefit is called Permanent Partial Disability (PPD) benefits. After you've continued to treat with a doctor for a period of time and the doctor has pretty much nothing else that they can do to treat your injury, they're going to list you as maximum medical improvement status. What that really means is there's nothing else that they can do to treat you. You're as good as you're going to be. At that point the doctor is going to assign you a percentage of your disability. So let's just say you've injured your back at work and the doctor is gone through the course of treatment and the doctor believes you've lost 10% of the use of your body or back due to the injury. That 10% gets thrown into a calculation and it comes out to a value that the insurance company owes you due to the loss of the percentage of the use of your body.

Those are the three income benefits. Now, you can also receive medical benefits. Medical benefits encompass exactly what it sounds like. Medical treatment from the employer and insurance company. Those benefits include all special procedures that a doctor may recommend for treatment - and include physical therapy, surgeries (if they're recommended), injections if they are recommended, and prescription pills. Even travel to and from your doctors' offices and to the pharmacy to pick up your prescriptions are benefits that are covered. Now obviously the medical benefits are paid directly to the person who is providing you the treatment. However, the mileage reimbursement is something that's yours and yours alone.

The third type of benefit that an injured worker receives, is in the unfortunate event for if someone passes away due to their injury which are death benefits. Death benefits encompass the cost of funeral expenses and if there is a living minor child or perhaps a spouse, they may be due the Income benefits that I've already discussed and that would have been due to the person who has passed away from their injury. So those are the three core benefits that anyone who has been injured in Georgia with a company with workers' compensation insurance. Those are the three types of benefits that someone is due.

Do's for Injured Workers:
Report Your Injury Immediately
Atlanta Workers Compensation Attorney

https://www.youtube.com/watch?v=oH8pMXjeAN0

Interviewer:

And there you have it. Right now we are learning more about Workers' Compensation 101 with Atty. Andre' Ramsay, who's Of Council with the Cochran Firm Atlanta. Mr. Ramsay, let's move forward and talk about the Do's and the Don'ts. What should an injured worker do?

Mr. Ramsay:

The very first thing an injured worker should do is report your injury to your supervisor immediately. If your supervisor is not available find a team lead. If your team leads aren't available find a manager. If they're not available, find an HR representative.

The point is you need to inform someone who is in a position of power with your employer immediately. Not only that you've been injured but that you've been injured due to your work or work environment.

It's not enough just to tell them I don't feel well or I'm having some pain. You have to let them know that this was caused while you were working or while you're at work. You need to do both of those things. So it needs to be happening while you're at work and, again, because of work. I cannot stress enough - report your injury immediately.

The law does allow you 30 days to provide notice to your employer of your injury but why wait? The longer you wait the longer it's going to take them to get you to a doctor for treatment. The real goal here is to inform the insurer and the employer rather quickly of your injury but the bigger goal is to get you to a doctor more quickly so that you can get better. That's the very first thing I would say you should do.

Do's for Injured Workers:
Call an Attorney Immediately
Workers' Compensation Attorney Atlanta

https://www.youtube.com/watch?v=O2z1c4zOXnM

Interviewer:

When should they call an attorney?

Mr. Ramsay:

They should call an attorney immediately after they've informed their employer. If you call an attorney prior to informing employer that's the first thing an attorney is going to tell you, so go ahead and inform the employer right away. Then the employer will inform the insurance company that represents them of the work compensation injury. Then you need to call an attorney immediately. Don't wait until the employer decides to say, "Okay, I'll send you to a doctor".

The reason I tell you call an attorney rather quickly it's because in workers' compensation it matters who the doctor is. It's sad and unfortunate. But not every doctor is there to provide you the benefits or the treatment that you need. A lot of doctors may push to get you back to work quicker than you are ready for. It's very important that you not only get a doctor but that you get the right doctor. That's what attorneys do. We get you to the right doctor, for the right treatment, to give you the right result.

Do's for Injured Workers:
Ask for an Incident Report
Atlanta Workers Comp Attorney

https://www.youtube.com/watch?v=OHG4Hl1TOjM

Interviewer:

What's the next thing that an injured worker should do?

Mr. Ramsay:

Ask for an incident report to be written up. I cannot stress to you how important that is. That's simply just documents about the injury. I've had cases in the past where the injured worker did in fact report the injury to the supervisor immediately. However, because an incident report wasn't written up or filed, the insurance company was not made aware of the injury in the beginning. So what that does is delay your treatment. It delays the income benefits and the medical treatment that you're due. So ask for an incident report to be filed, then ask for a copy because you are due a copy of that report. Not a lot of employers will give you a copy if you choose not to ask for it to be filed within your records. That way, when your attorney is on the record, he or she can go ahead and request a copy of your entire employment record - which would include that work injury claim form. So again, ask for an incident report to be written up, filed, and ask for a copy of the bill.

Interviewer:

What should an injured worker do if they have a preexisting injury?

Mr. Ramsay:

Listen, preexisting injuries are fine. No one expects you to be free of all preexisting injuries. If you've been hurt before then that's okay. What we need to show and establish is that your pre-existing injury has been aggravated due to the work that you are performing for your employer. As long as we could show that it's been aggravated to some degree, then your claim will, and still should be accepted as a workers' compensation claim. I would say 80-90% of my clients have had preexisting injuries so it is not a big deal claiming workers' compensation. Unfortunately a lot of employers and insurance companies will use that as a tool to not provide you the treatment that you need. They'll simply say, "Oh, this is something you had before you came to work so this is not our problem". Again, another reason why you need to call an attorney immediately especially if you had a preexisting injury. Just to reiterate, preexisting injuries do not bar you from filing the workers' compensation claim nor bar you from receiving the income benefits or the medical treatment that you need. It is very important to get an attorney as soon as possible in the event that your employer and/or your insurance company denies your claims simply because you've been hurt before. I will say this, it does get problematic at times if your pre-existing injury is within, let's say, a month from your date of injury. That gives the employer/insurance company another tool to deny you treatment. So again, another reason I cannot stress enough to call an attorney as soon as you've been hurt.

Interviewer:

What's the next thing that an injured worker should do?

Mr. Ramsay:

After you've reported to your supervisor and you've asked for an incident report to be filed and written up, ask for medical treatment. It seems simple, but a lot of times I've had cases where my injured workers inform the employer, have the incident written up and then go home and try to see if going home for a day or two will make him feel better. It's not enough just to do that. You need to be proactive about your care and proactive about your treatment - ask for medical treatment. When you ask for a medical treatment then at that point, the employer is supposed to provide you with a list of doctors, it's called a "panel of physicians". The panel by Georgia law is supposed to have at minimum six doctors in which you could request treatment. If the panel does not have six doctors then that panel may be deemed as invalid. If it is invalid, then you get to pick whichever doctor you want to go to and the employer/ insurance company will have to pay for the treatment. Be mindful that the employer's/insurance will not just allow you to go to any doctor you want and agree to pay for everything which is another reason why you need an attorney to assist you with this.

When you ask for treatment let's just assume that the panel is valid. You get to pick whichever doctor you want to go to. What happens quite frequently, is the employer or insurer will tell you, you need to go to this particular place or you need to go to that particular place. There are a lot of reasons behind that, but all those reasons do not benefit you. The first reason is that they are very familiar with that doctor and know that the doctor might send you back to work before you need to be back to work or state that there's nothing wrong with you or that you're fine. You need to make sure you're going again to not only a doctor but the right doctor. You need a doctor that specializes in your type of injury and you need a doctor that's going to provide you unbiased care in an unbiased treatment plan and with an unbiased diagnosis. Again, ask for medical treatment, ask for the list of doctors so you can pick which doctor - and before you pick a doctor, call an attorney - let's pick the right doctor and let's start your claim off your right.

Do's for Injured Workers:
Secure Contact Info For Witnesses
Georgia Workers Compensation Lawyer

https://www.youtube.com/watch?v=y5sWER24X0k

Interviewer:

So what's the next thing that an injured worker should do?

Mr. Ramsay:

The next thing you should do is secure contact information for witnesses that may have seen your accident. Anyone that you work with, coworkers, see if they can write something down for you. Just say, "I know you saw this happen, and saw the circumstances of my injury. Could you report that me, the injured worker, was doing so-and-so work activity and then complained of back pain (or shoulder pain or ankle pain or hand pain, etc)".

You always want to secure people that might support you. The reason why is quite simple. The more people that saw the accident, the more chances that it's going to be a claim that's accepted; more chances that the insurance company will send you to a doctor for treatment and pay for it; more chances that you will receive the income benefit should you have to miss work.

This is information that is typically going to be placed on your incident report which brings us right back to why you want to have an incident report in the first place - You want to identify those people that would provide you information and provided the insurance company information to give them a reason to accept your claim and provide you the treatment that you need. It doesn't have to be a formal statement by someone as a witness you work with them (or your friends at work), but try to get something in writing and see if they'll agree to sign it. Let them know it won't affect their jobs initially. You'll only use it if absolutely necessary. But it's very good to have it while the information is current in their head - especially right after the accident so they can accurately represent what they saw versus asking them to make a statement some two to three weeks, or even two to three months, later. It's very important to secure the contact information for those witnesses and see if they'll provide you with a statement.

Don'ts for Injured Workers:
Don't Sign Anything
Workers' Compensation Lawyer Atlanta

https://www.youtube.com/watch?v=R083aUr4_7E

Interviewer:

Now, Mr. Ramsay, let's go into the don'ts for injured workers. What is something that they should not do?

Mr. Ramsay:

I tell everyone, do not sign anything before you speak with an attorney. About the only thing that you may sign is the incident report that we discussed. Make sure it's an accurate representation of what happened and how it happened. If you don't agree with it, you don't have to sign it. They may try to force you to do so, but tell them you want to speak to an attorney before you sign, especially if it's not accurate.

Don't sign anything regarding which doctors you're going to go see.

Don't sign anything regarding how the accident happened from the insurance company.

Don't sign anything before you can get the medical treatment you need.

By the time your income benefits are due, you should have already obtained an attorney that can help you and make sure the right paperwork is signed but only after an attorney has had the opportunity to review those documents and make sure they don't prohibit you from receiving the benefits that you're due or may negatively impact your claim, and/or your treatment going forward.

You have to be very careful with the things that you sign because you may lock yourself into something that's not beneficial to you well before you've had the chance to really review it or to really appreciate the severity of your injury.

Especially, do not sign anything if you're under the influence of any type of prescription pills, or if you're in an ambulance. Unfortunately it has happened to one of my clients where the employer asked him to sign something when she was being loaded onto an ambulance. Then we get into issues where the paperwork that she signed may not even be valid due to the stress of the situation that you are under. To avoid that whole argument entirely, it is best you don't sign anything without speaking to an attorney. We need to make sure that what you sign, benefits you and only you. A lot of times what you sign may benefit the employer and you don't even know it yet because you haven't appreciated the severity of your injury and neither had your employer.

Don'ts for Injured Workers:
Don't Wait to Report Your Injury
Workers' Compensation Atlanta

https://www.youtube.com/watch?v=KaWtH_q65vE

Interviewer:

What happens if an injured worker waits to report an injury?

Mr.Ramsay:

It's quite simple. You're denying yourself the availability of treatment. The longer you wait - the longer it is going to take for you to get better; for you to get back to work; and for you to provide the income for your family. I cannot stress enough - It's detrimental to your claim not to report right away. Earlier I indicated that you have thirty days to report your injury and that is true, but why wait thirty days? I understand there are certain times that you don't appreciate perhaps how bad your back hurts, or that some injuries take time to appreciate to a level to where you feel like you need treatment. That's why the law allows you thirty days. However, the longer you wait to do so then you're putting yourself in a position to where the insurance company could deny your claim - not because you haven't provided the notice within thirty days - but because they just flat out don't believe you. They might simply ask you, "Well, why did you wait so long if you're in such excruciating pain.". Don't give the employer or the insurance company a reason to back out of providing you the treatment. Tell them what happened, report the injury, get incident report and ask for treatment as soon as possible.

If you do wait after the thirty days then 99% of the time the insurance company will deny your claim because they don't have to provide treatment after the thirty days. It gives them a way to back out of the treatment. There may be ways around that thirty day notice period and that's what attorneys do to make sure that your claim gets accepted. But again, if you do not have to put yourself in a bad position then don't do so.

The beginning of your claim is a very very important time frame. That's why there are statutory time frames when you need to report your claim. So the faster you can do that and the faster we can get you the right treatment, the faster we can get your income benefits, with no interruption in the income that comes into your household and the faster we can just put you in a better position and you were at the time of the injury. So don't wait. Report it. Ask for the incident report to be written up, and ask for treatment as soon as possible.

Don'ts for Injured Workers:
Don't Try To Do Your Claim By Yourself
Georgia Workers' Comp

https://www.youtube.com/watch?v=St2wcR04-3Q

Interviewer:

All right. So we have our Workers' Compensation 101 Do's and Don'ts and now we're talking about the Don'ts. What's next on the list?

Mr. Ramsay:

I would say don't try to do your claim by yourself. I understand in a perfect world your employer will provide you the benefit, and the medical treatment that you need; and if you miss time from work, they'll provide you the income benefits. Most people really don't want to file claims against their employer. They really just want to hope that the employer "does right by them". Don't put yourself in that position. I cannot tell you how many clients have signed up with me after they attempted to give their employer a way to try to make things right. But keep in mind when you get injured at work, you're no longer only dealing with you and your employer; You're not dealing with the people that you're familiar with; You're not dealing with your employer/H.R. department or your manager who you've worked for for forty years or ten years. Who you're really dealing with is the insurance company. They have no idea who you are. To them you're simply a stack of paper

- You're a claim number - You're a unit. They are going to treat you as such if you let them treat you as such.

This is very important to understand if you don't try to do this by yourself. Why? Because this is probably their first or second time ever having someone being hurt at work. Most people never get hurt at work. So they're never put in that situation. You're going into this by yourself with no prior experience. Meanwhile the insurance company have had three to four hundred claims on their desk at any given time. Your case, like every other case, is them just simply trying to move the file along, and it gets you subpar treatment. If they get you back to work and then the claim is moved off of their desk. Don't put yourself in this position - You're putting yourself at detriment already by trying to do the claim by yourself.

I cannot tell you how many people tried to do it themselves and then they call me and say, "I wish I didn't do it by myself". Don't be like people who call me all the time asking me to fix things. I try my best to fix whatever the situation is and I do my best to put you in a better situation but if you can call a lawyer first, you can get your claim done the right way from the beginning. It will go much smoother and get you to the right doctors. With an attorney you will get the income benefits versus if you try to do it by yourself.

You may be seen as a detriment, and the employer may consider terminating you for whatever reason and then after you're trying to file a claim. It just pushes you into a lawsuit - It puts you behind the eight ball and slows down your treatment. It gives the employer/insurance company a reason to deny your claim and not provide you anything so that the only person that suffers is you. Do not try to do this by yourself. You have a friend in the business - I'm your friend. The Cochran firm here is your friend in the business. We could do what we need to do to try to help you get where you need to be because nobody is looking out for your best interests except you…and your attorney.

Don'ts for Injured Workers:
Don't Accept Settlements
Atlanta Workers' Compensation Lawyer

https://www.youtube.com/watch?v=af2_-Wa2LD0

Interviewer:

Let's talk next about settlement money…

Mr. Ramsay:

One thing I always tell my clients, if the insurance company makes you an offer before you even ask for money don't accept it - because at that point they're offering you a very minimal amount of money. It may seem like a lot to you and if it does, it's because the claim is really worth a lot more and they know it. So don't accept any settlement monies in lieu of filing for treatment or filing a claim.

I've seen that happen before - I've seen a client of mine who worked in a warehouse and injured his back severely. The employer asked him, "Look, let's not file a claim. We'll take care of all your medical treatment or we'll give you some money ahead of time so you can take care of everything you need to do…Let's not get our insurance company involved."

Don't do that to yourself. What you're doing is leaving your future in the hands of somebody who doesn't care about your future. The only reason that they don't want you to file a claim is because they don't want to provide you the real treatment that you need. They simply don't want their insurance premiums to go up. Workers' compensation insurance premiums are pretty much like an auto insurance premium that you and I pay every day. When you get injured and are in a car accident - If someone hits you from the rear and they come up and say exactly the same thing to you. "Hey! Let's not get our insurance company involved" - Do you feel comfortable going forward without calling the insurance company? Of course not. The reason you don't feel comfortable is because you have no idea who that person is that hit you. You have no idea what their intentions are and you do not know whether they will provide you the treatment that you need. That's the exact same scenario for the insurance company for your workers' compensation.

Remember, again - When you're filing a claim you're dealing with the insurance company not the employer. There is no good reason your employer can give you for not filing a claim with their insurance companies. They pay premiums for a reason. Let the specialist do what they do. Do not accept any type of monies in lieu of treatment or filing a claim because whatever money you may accept, I promise you this, it will not be enough. You will be on the hook for your own treatment. Simple things like physical therapy cost hundreds of tens of dollars per session typically. If you need thirty treatments or thirty sessions of physical therapy that's thirty hundred dollar payments.

We haven't even gotten into whether you need surgery. We haven't gotten into specialized care with orthopedic specialist, neurologist or psychiatrist. There are so many avenues that you're eliminating if you simply accept money in lieu of treatment and or filing a claim. There's no way you can appreciate the severity of your injury immediately in the first ten days or so after your accident. These things take time.

Give yourself the opportunity to get the treatment you need. To find out what is going on with your body and to find out what it is that you're going to need for the rest of your life. That's what we do here. We appreciate the severity of all the injuries that we represent for our clients and we try to put them in a better position that will allow us to do what we can to put you in a good position. If you accept money in the beginning, in lieu of treatment and or filing a claim, then you're handcuffing yourself to do whatever you "accept" and it's going to be grossly undervalue.

Don't Decide to Seek Treatment With Your Own Health Coverage Workers' Compensation Lawyers Atlanta

https://www.youtube.com/watch?v=qasI8Xv2VNU

Interviewer:

What is our final Don't with the Workers' Compensation 101 Do's and Don'ts?

Mr. Ramsay:

Don't decide to only seek treatment with your own primary care physician with your own health coverage. I understand you're familiar and happy with the doctors who have been treating you for some ten to twenty years so you're more comfortable going that route. The problem with that is the insurance company doesn't care who your primary care physician is. Insurance companies want you to go to a doctor that is an authorized treating physician. As a matter of fact, the law says that you specifically need to go to an authorized treating physician.

Who is an authorized treating physician? Let's back it up to the panel of physicians that we discussed earlier. The panel of physicians is any doctor you pick off of that list. The list should be a minimum of six doctors who are authorized as treating physicians for your workers' compensation injury. If you choose to bypass those doctors and go directly to your doctor, you're putting yourself at risk and you're putting your claim at risk because now we don't have someone who is authorized as your treating physician diagnosing what your injury is or stating what your treatment plan is. When a doctor is not authorized, guess who's footing the bill? You are. That means you could go and get this treatment that cost tens of thousands of dollars and there is nothing your attorney can do to get that money back for you; you simply didn't go to the doctor that you needed to go to.

I completely understand when you are injured that you want to go to somebody you trust. That's why it's important to trust your attorney - because your attorney sees this on a daily basis and knows how you feel. We try to get you to the right doctors that we know will mesh well you and the paying insurance company. Your attorney will know the physicians who will provide an unbiased treatment plan and if they can not treat you for your injuries, then they'll refer you to people who can.

Don't rely on your own doctors, or your own primary care physicians before you go to a workers' compensation doctor. There may be ways in which your attorney can get your authorized treating physician as your primary care physician. But it won't happen until you give us an opportunity to look at your case. If we do that, we can get your primary care physician to be your authorized treating physician and then everybody's going to be happy. You'll be with who you need to be with and who you're comfortable with. If they provide appropriate care then the insurance company will pay for it.

Give us the opportunity to help you immediately after your injury and if your employer is not trying to send you to a doctor immediately and you want to go see your own doctor, then your attorney will try and get you that. If you are in pain, don't stay in pain. As a matter of fact, you can even go to the emergency room if you're in severe pain - at least initially. But don't continue to treat with those doctors unilaterally until you go to a workers' compensation doctor or you will put your claim at risk. We'll get you to the right doctors; we'll get you the right care; we'll get you the right treatment that will put you in the right position.

Workers' Compensation Attorney:
Do's and Don'ts for Injured Workers

https://www.youtube.com/watch?v=KfKpUTdmCtE

Interviewer:

And there you have it, Workers Compensation 101; Workers' Compensation Do's and Don'ts for injured workers; Again this is Atty. Andre' Ramsay with the Cochran Firm Atlanta, Workers' Compensation. Thank you so much for sharing so much valuable information with us today. We appreciate it Mr. Ramsay.

Mr. Ramsay:

It was my pleasure. I fight for the injured workers on a daily basis. That's what we do here at the Cochran Firm. I truly feel like it's my calling and my focus is on educating the client. I want to educate you you to be aware of what your rights are so no one pulls the wool over your eyes.

It won't happen with me on your side. I've been an attorney for workers' comp for quite a while. Prior to being an attorney, I worked in call centers, warehouses, retail…I've done it all. These are the things that make me passionate about helping you because I have walked in your shoes. Things like this there are great because it gives me a platform to speak and provide information freely that people need. If they ever need to call me, I'm always available to discuss their situation with them and provide a free consultation to answer specific questions.

Interviewer:

Well, there it is. If you're facing a legal issue and need help, please contact Mr. Andre' Ramsay at the Cochran Firm Atlanta. There's no fee or obligation for the first consultation and you can also find more information at workerscompensationanswers.com where there is a full video library with dozens of videos to help you make an informed decision or find out more information about the firm.

What Income Benefits
Are Injured Workers Entitled?

https://www.youtube.com/watch?v=OKGCogYajxI

I'm Attorney Andre' Ramsay, your workers' compensation attorney. Let's talk a little bit about income benefits that you deserve when you are hurt at work. Workers' compensation insurance companies are to pay you two-thirds of your average weekly wage when you cannot return to work due to your injuries. Now, let's just say you are a pilot and you earn over $100,000 a year. Now you earn about $28,000 a year. That's a huge difference and that's why you need an attorney to help you. Let's just say you earn $550 a week. Now you earn about $400 a week. The income benefits do reduce but your bills do not, and that's why we're here to try to assist you. Again, I'm Andre' Ramsay, the lawyer for the everyday worker.

When Does An Employer Need To Carry Workers' Comp Insurance?

https://www.youtube.com/watch?v=tZ8RsD607d8

I'm Attorney Andre' Ramsay, your workers' compensation attorney. When does an employer need to carry workers' compensation insurance in Georgia? It's quite simple. If they do business in the State of Georgia and they have more than three employees, then they are required by the state to carry workers' compensation insurance. So don't let an employer fool you by telling you that they don't carry workers' compensation insurance. Give us a call and let us help you figure it out, and let's represent you and get you the insurance benefits that you need. I am Andre' Ramsay, the lawyer for the everyday worker.

Why Do You Need
A Workers' Compensation Attorney?

https://www.youtube.com/watch?v=1ClK7Sms6Tg

I'm Attorney Andre' Ramsay, your workers' compensation attorney. Why do you need an attorney? It's because the insurance company knows that if you don't have an attorney, they could take full advantage of you, and they won't give you the benefits that you deserve: income benefits, medical benefits. Those are just the beginning of the things that they owe you. But you won't know if you simply look it up on Google. Give us a call today so we could try to figure out what is best for you, and hopefully I can be the attorney that helps you get what you need. I'm Andre' Ramsay, the lawyer for the everyday worker.

How Soon Can You Get To The Doctor?

https://www.youtube.com/watch?v=dRea_LjndFg

I'm Attorney Andre' Ramsay, your workers' compensation attorney. Now how soon should you get to the doctor? Immediately. If you need medical treatment, don't wait. It's not about being a lawyer talking to his client, it's about being a person first. If you need the medical treatment, don't wait. Your family needs you. First thing you should do, contact your employer, inform them of your injury and ask them to go see a workers' compensation doctor. But if you need emergency services, then simply go to the emergency room. I've had clients who have had the ambulance come and pick them up and take them to the hospital. Your health and well being means more. Get the treatment that you need. So do not wait. Go immediately to the emergency room or go to the workers' compensation doctor as soon as possible. And if you need to, you can see your personal primary care physician. But always go first to either the emergency room or to the workers' compensation doctors. Again, I am Andre' Ramsay, the lawyer for the everyday worker.

What Medical Benefits
Are Injured Workers Entitled?

https://www.youtube.com/watch?v=vQVh1LAOjog

Hi, I'm Attorney Andre' Ramsay, your workers' compensation attorney. Let's talk a little bit about medical benefits that you deserve when you're hurt at work. Your employer by law is supposed to list a panel of physicians, perhaps on a bulletin board, maybe in a lunch room. That panel of physicians has to list at minimum six doctors for you to choose where you'd like to go for treatment. That panel is supposed to have a minimum one orthopedic specialist, at maximum two industrial clinics, such as a Concentra or a Caduceus and other doctors that can provide you some treatment. Don't let them send you to a doctor they're familiar with and you are not with. Those doctors control the medical, which means they could return you to work sooner than you need to be. That's why you need us to help you get the right doctors to get you the right treatment to put you where you need to be. The ultimate goal here is to get better. Once you're better, you're able to return to work, you're able to provide for your families. Let us help you get there. Again, I'm Andre' Ramsay, the lawyer for the everyday worker.

What Kind of Benefits Do Injured Workers Received?

https://www.youtube.com/watch?v=gNQr4Be7oxc

Hi, I'm Attorney Andre' Ramsay, your workers' compensation attorney. What kind of benefits do injured workers receive when they're hurt at work? Three types of benefits. First, they get medical benefits which is probably more important to you. Second type of benefit, income benefits and third, unfortunately, if the person passed away at work then they get death benefits. We'll discuss this a little bit more as we talk about the three types of benefits. Again, income benefits, medical benefits and death benefits. I'm Andre' Ramsay, the lawyer for the everyday worker.

What Does No Fault Liability Mean?

https://www.youtube.com/watch?v=kL6NeDMMzEg

Hi. I'm Attorney Andre' Ramsay, your workers' compensation attorney. What does no fault liability mean? Georgia's a no fault state when people get hurt at work. Now, what that really means is we're not considering negligence of third parties. We're not considering your own negligence that caused your injury and we're not considering the employer's negligence that caused your injury. So it really doesn't matter how your injury occurred. It matters that it occurred at work and it mattered that it occurred due to you performing work for your employer. That's it. You meet those two prongs, you turn into an injured worker that needs help, and that's what we're here for. We provide you the medical benefits and the income benefits that you deserve. We fight for people like you every day because we're just like you. We work hard. We get injured. We need the benefits just like you do. Again, I am Andre' Ramsay, the lawyer for the everyday worker.

What Death Benefits
Are Injured Workers Entitled?

https://www.youtube.com/watch?v=nnKtuwpalnE

Hi. I'm Attorney Andre' Ramsay, your workers' compensation attorney. Let's talk a little bit about death benefits. If an injured worker dies due to performing work within the State of Georgia for an employer, his family is due death benefits. Now, what are those? Death benefits include funeral expenses, and in some instances, workers' compensation has to pay the income benefits the deceased would have received to his or her family members. Let us help you receive the income benefits that you deserve for your loved one that has passed away. That is what we do. Again, I am Andre' Ramsay, the lawyer for the everyday worker.

What Happens
If You Have a Preexisting Injury?

https://www.youtube.com/watch?v=_IPKw98MJRA

Hi, I'm Attorney Andre' Ramsay, your workers' compensation attorney. Now I hear this question all the time, what if I have a pre-existing injury? Tell you what folks, I have a pre-existing injury. Most people do. It happens. Workers' compensation doesn't eliminate you from receiving any benefits simply because you've been hurt before. People go through things every day and if you're a worker, you've been injured at some point and some time of your life. So workers' compensation still provides you the income benefits and still the medical benefits that you deserve. Don't let an employer tell you simply because you've had a pre-existing injury that you don't qualify for such. It's a well-known tactic for employers and a very well-known tactic for insurance companies. Don't let them fool you. Give us a call. Let us help you with that because that's what we do every day. I've helped thousands of injured workers and 90% of them have had pre-existing injuries. It means absolutely nothing. At the end of the day, you still get the benefits that you deserve. Let us help you. Again, I'm Andre' Ramsay, the lawyer for the everyday worker.

Does It Matter
If the Injury Is Your Fault?

https://www.youtube.com/watch?v=OrF7A7LUhh4

Hi, I am attorney Andre' Ramsay; your workers' compensation attorney. Now does it matter if the injury was your fault? Short answer, not typically. There are some instances where if you're actually horsing around or doing willful misconduct that is against the policy of your employer then it may not be covered by workers' compensation insurance. But in the vast majority of instances, even if the injury was your fault, you still get coverage. It is still a workers' compensation case, it is still an instance in which you still deserve those medical benefits that you need and you still get those income benefits as well.

Let us help you with that. A lot of these things are facts specific so we need all the information in order to tell you specifically if you're covered. But again, in a vast majority of instances, it matters not if you caused your own injury. Georgia is a no fault State when it comes to workers' compensation. So negligence on your part is not as big as an issue as you make think it is.

Give us a call, let us help you. Again, I am Andre' Ramsay, the lawyer for the everyday worker.

What Should You Do After An Injury at Work?

https://www.youtube.com/watch?v=J6sdzFcipPo

Hi. I'm Attorney Andre' Ramsay, your workers' compensation attorney.

Now, what should you do after you suffer an injury at work? It's quite simple - tell someone, whether it's your team lead, whether it's your supervisor, your supervisor's supervisor. But inform someone not only that you are hurt, but also that you were hurt because of work. That's very important. By law, you have 30 days to provide your employer with notice of an injury. I implore you not to wait for 30 days, sooner the better. Tell them right away. That way, an incident report can be written up. That way, you can get to the medical treatment that you need sooner than later. And that way, there is not possibly an investigation that would stop you from getting the benefits that you deserve.

So again, inform your supervisor immediately after the injury. If you have to go to the emergency room immediately, then do so. But after you get home from the emergency room, call your supervisor, call your employer, and keep a written report or a record of what happened. Try to fill out an Incident Report if needed. Most employers would appreciate you doing so because then there's record of the injury. Do all of these things and also don't forget to call me. I'm here to help you with your injury. I'm here to help you with your accident. That is what I do. Again, my name is Andre' Ramsay and I'm the lawyer for the everyday worker.

How Much Is Your
Workers' Compensation Case Worth?

https://www.youtube.com/watch?v=MwHjzKkupvk

Hi. I'm Attorney Andre' Ramsay, your workers' compensation attorney. I get asked all the time, "How much is my workers' compensation case worth?" The truth is, it depends. Before I answer that question, let me tell me you how a workers' compensation case is different from any other case, specifically a slip and fall or personal injury case. Workers' compensation does not award injured workers pain and suffering. Now, I know you've been through it. I can only imagine.

You've been through some pain, you've been through some suffering, and you probably still will go through that no matter what happens with your case. But it's important to realize that there is no value in workers' compensation for pain and suffering. Now, injuries cost based off of the type of injury it is. For instance, if it's a back injury, it may have more value than an ankle injury or perhaps a hand injury, right? To know the true answer, it's based off of how much you make on a weekly basis and how much the insurance company owes you if you're out of work for a period of time.

There are three things we consider in any workers' compensation settlement. The first, how much do they owe you on a weekly basis. Second, how much is needed for your future medical treatment and for how long. Third, what is your disability rating. Now, disability rating is typically assigned to you by workers' compensation doctor. But he or she won't assign that until you've been through some form of treatment for a period of time, and after you've reached what's called maximum medical improvement. That just simply means there is nothing else the doctor can do to put you in a better position. But due to your injury and your accident, you've lost a percentage of the use of your body due to the accident. Those three factors is what we take into consideration where we're coming up with any type of value.

The good thing about what we do at the Cochran Firm is, I will always contact you and discuss with you what your claim is worth, well before I submit a demand to the insurance company. So you and I will have a good understanding of where your case is, how much its worth, and more importantly, how much the insurance company will pay. So give me a call today. Let's discuss your treatment as well as your settlement options. Again, I'm Andre' Ramsay, the lawyer for the everyday worker.

When Should You Contact A Workers' Compensation Attorney?

https://www.youtube.com/watch?v=CiWUD1xT3OY

Hi. I'm Attorney Andre' Ramsay, your workers' compensation attorney. Now, when should you actually contact an attorney? You should contact one immediately. First, always contact your employer to a formal of the entry. Second, contact a doctor so you can get a treatment. And third, contact us. Now, the employer may not want you to actually acquire an attorney. The insurance company certainly would prefer that you do this alone. They could take advantage of you by giving you little to know treatment, providing you little to know income benefits and simply doing with you what they do with thousands of people who tried to do it alone. Don't be the next victim. Call your attorney immediately. Again, I'm Andre' Ramsay, the lawyer for the everyday worker.

How Do You Pay Your Workers' Compensation Attorney?
https://www.youtube.com/watch?v=JqO9Uw8rwug

Hi. I'm Attorney Andre' Ramsay, your workers' compensation attorney. This question is typically the third question I get. First question is always, how do I get medical treatment? Second question, how do I get income benefits? But this particular question, how do I pay my attorney? We get paid off for contingency basis, similar to a person and your client. What that means is, you don't owe me a dime until you get your result. Settlement, is the only way that we get paid. If your claim doesn't settle, you don't owe us anything. That's the risk we take. That's the risk we feel we are able to take because we are invest in you. Let us help you get better and let us help you get the money that you deserve. Again, I'm Attorney Andre' Ramsay and I'm the lawyer for the everyday worker.

How Long Does the Process Take for Your Workers' Compensation Claim?

https://www.youtube.com/watch?v=F_RzRFUPo4U

Hi. I'm Attorney Andre' Ramsay, your workers' compensation attorney. How long does your workers' compensation claim take? It's simple. It takes as long as it needs to. I've had claims that are going on for a week, a month. I've had claims going on for two or three years. I have a client right now who is in due back at 1999 and she still has a workers' compensation claim. If you need treatment, then we take as long as we need to to make sure you got a treatment that you deserve in order to get better, in order to return to work. If you look into settle your claim, then perhaps you wanna short a time frame to working with this compensation claim. We can discuss that. But it moves as you needed to move. Give us a call. I'll talk to you be more specific about what needs to be done for your claim and what needs to be done to get you what you need to be. Again, I'm Andre' Ramsay, the lawyer for the everyday worker.

How Long Do You File A Workers' Compensation Claim in Georgia?

https://www.youtube.com/watch?v=JSvxjd3P5NU

Hi, I'm Attorney Andre' Ramsay. Your workers' compensation attorney, now how long do you have to file a claim within the State of Georgia?

State of Georgia allows you one year from the date of injury to file a claim. If the claim is being controverted, meaning if the employer's not providing any income or medical benefits, you've got the one year from your date of injury.

Now, if the employer and the insurance company is actually providing you medical benefits only, then you have one year from the last date of medical treatment in order to file a claim in the State of Georgia. If the employer or the insurer is providing you medical benefits, at least initially, then you have two years from the last date of any income benefits proceed in order to file a claim with the State of Georgia.

Now don't be confused. You can actually file a claim with your insurance company and not file a claim with the State of Georgia. Many injured workers believe simply because they file a claim with the insurance company, then that's it. That is not final end all be all. You need to also file a claim with the State of Georgia to inform the State of Georgia that you've been hurt and that you're receiving income benefits or that you need those income benefits that the employer has denied you.

All of these sounds like a lot of information and it is. That's why it's all over the internet. But more importantly, that's why you need us. Let us help you. Don't do this alone.

Again, I'm Andre' Ramsay, the lawyer for the everyday worker.

Can Independent Contractors Get Workers' Compensation?

https://www.youtube.com/watch?v=BRdw-_dbJXc

Hi, I'm Attorney Andre' Ramsay, your workers' compensation attorney. Now Georgia workers' compensation insurance typically covers employees of employers, meaning you're someone that works there on an everyday basis. You're getting paid by the company. They tell you what to do and how to do it.

But what if you're an independent contractor? Well sometimes we could still get those benefits that you deserve, simply just titling you as an independent contractor doesn't relieve the employer from all liability they have if you're injured at work.

There's certain things that you need to consider when you're an independent contractor. Do you use your own tools or do they provide you with tools? Do they tell you when to come into work or do you set your own schedule? Do they tell you how and when to do your work or do you do that?

There's so many factors to consider when you're an independent contractor, that you need the services of an attorney to make sure that you're protected. Don't just listen to the employer when they tell you, "Well you're an independent contractor. You're not covered." I've had many clients, specifically clients who work for construction companies who are working for a contractor or a subcontractor. I've been able to get those benefits for them because they knew they needed an attorney. They contacted an attorney and we got them the benefits that they need.

So don't do this by yourself. The law is topsy and turvy when it comes to independent contractors and employers.

Please give me a call and let's discuss it. I give a free consultation, so you won't owe me any money just to discuss.

Again, I'm Andre' Ramsay, the lawyer for the everyday worker.

When Do You Start Getting Your Income Benefits?

https://www.youtube.com/watch?v=X6wl1_V_898

Hi, I'm Attorney Andre' Ramsay, your workers' compensation attorney. Now the question is when do I start getting my income benefits?

Georgia requires that you wait a seven-day waiting period before you start receiving income benefits. Now, typically that means on the eighth day you would be due benefits, doesn't mean necessarily that you will receive them on the eighth day. The insurance company has twenty-one days before they decide whether they're going to pick your claim up, meaning that they're going to pay you your income benefits or whether they are going to deny the claim.

So your first check is actually not due until that twenty-one day period is up. Now if you're out of work for the entire twenty-one days, you get all twenty-one days worth of time that you've missed. But if you're before that twenty-one day period, they only owe you after that eighth day that you're out of work. I know it's a lot of dates. It sounds very complex because it is. That's why you need us to help.

So give us a call. Let us get you the benefits you need and let's get them for you for fast, because you need them now.

Again, my name is Andre' Ramsay and I'm the lawyer for the everyday worker.

What Happens If You Wait To Report Your Injury?

https://www.youtube.com/watch?v=dX_pFtDKuvg

Hi, I'm Attorney Andre' Ramsay, your workers' compensation attorney. Now what happens if you wait to report your injury? By law, Georgia allows you thirty days to provide notice to your employer, not only about the injury but that the injury occurred at or because of work. If you wait after thirty days, you're essentially leaving yourself in a position in where your claim will be denied by the insurance companies. Don't give them a reason to do so. Notify your employer, whether it's your supervisor, your team lead, immediately after the injury. It makes sense.

Get your benefits now. Why wait thirty days to go get treatment? You need to get better, now, not later.

Again, my name is Andre' Ramsay, and I'm the lawyer for the everyday worker.

If You Don't File a Workers' Compensation Claim Will You Stay Employed?

https://www.youtube.com/watch?v=TeR3tw2NOnY

Hi, I'm Attorney Andre' Ramsay, your workers' compensation attorney. I get asked this question all the time."Can my employer fire me?" The answer, absolutely yes. Georgia is an at-will State, so your employer can fire you for any or no reason at all. I've had one client who was terminated because she simply went to the restroom. Had another client that was terminated because he showed up one minute late.

You will find that the employer-employee relationship changes when you get injured at work. It matters not whether you filed your workers' compensation claim or not. So don't think because you do not follow workers' compensation claim that they'll keep you employed. You need to be protected. Do not do this alone. Let us help you. Again, my name is Andre' Ramsay and I'm the lawyer for the everyday worker.

What Happens If You Wait
To Report Your Injury?

https://www.youtube.com/watch?v=muoXui8w4qQ

Hi, I'm attorney Andre' Ramsay your workers' compensation attorney. What happens if you wait to report your injury? I had a client just like you, hardworking man. He worked for weeks and weeks and weeks thinking the pain in his elbow would go away, when it didn't, he sort to file it under workers' compensation, they immediately denied his claim because he waited three to four weeks to report his injury.

But the good news is that Georgia allows you 30 days to actually provide notice to your employer of the injury. Now what you cost yourself by waiting after 30 days is, they stand to deny your injury.

We can still help you even if they deny your injury, still call us but don't put yourself in that situation if you don't have to.

The first thing you need to do is call your employer and inform them of the injury. The second thing you need to do is ask to get seen by a workers' compensation doctor. The third thing you need to do is give us a call, we can take it from there.

Again, I'm Andre' Ramsay and I'm the lawyer for the everyday worker.

Can You File a Personal Injury Claim Against Your Employer?

https://www.youtube.com/watch?v=53IlWNxOL4g

Hi, I'm attorney Andre' Ramsay, your workers' compensation attorney. Now, when you get injured at work, can you file a personal injury claim against your employer? The answer is no.

Specifically, Georgia has workers' compensation law as an exclusive remedy for people who are injured at work. That does not mean, however, that you can't file a personal injury claim against a third party. Think about it.

I have a client who is a pizza delivery man. He was delivering pizza on his route. He gets rear-ended by the negligence of a third party. He has a workers' compensation claim against his employer to get the income and medical benefits that he needs, but he also has a personal injury claim against the third party that struck his vehicle.

So you keep it separate. A lot of times you can have multiple claims deriving from the same injury. But again, to answer your question; against your employer, you cannot bring a personal injury claim against them. It's very unfair but there are certain instances that we could try to find perhaps other claims that you may be able to bring against your employer, which is why you need to services of the Cochran Firm and myself.

So please, give us a call. Let's discuss it. We will find all avenues of claims and all avenues for recoveries for you. Again, my name is Andre' Ramsay and I'm the lawyer for the everyday worker.

How Much Does The Insurance Company Have to Pay An Injured Worker?

https://www.youtube.com/watch?v=t3zsNpJSKdw

Hi, I'm attorney Andre' Ramsay. Your workers' compensation attorney. Now, how much does an insurance company have to pay you while you are out of work? The answer is, it depends.

So, I based off of the calculation. Workers' compensation insurance companies have to pay you two thirds of the average weekly wage up to a maximum of $550. The maximum depends on your date of injury. That's why you need to call us so, we can let you know which date of injury falls under which maximum amount of income.

Now, that means if you are delta pilot and you earn $150 000 a year, now, based on income benefits that you're receiving from the insurance company, you're making about $28 000 a year. That's a huge bill to swallow. Which is why, you need us to help you.

Yeah so, if you are factory worker or are working in a plant, then your income benefits may significantly reduce based off of what is necessary for workers' compensation that pay you, because they only have to give you two thirds of your average weekly wage.

It makes a huge difference and we keep that in mind what we're fighting for you. Again, my name is Andre' Ramsay and I am a lawyer for the everyday worker.

What Happens After You Receive Medical Care?

https://www.youtube.com/watch?v=KwMSfmdIwno

Hi. I'm attorney Andre' Ramsay, your workers' compensation attorney. Now, what happens after you receive medical care? Follow through with the treatment that is recommended by your doctors. It's important to go not only to a doctor but to a Workers' Compensation doctor.

We've discussed this already, meaning the doctors listed on the panels of physicians. That's a workers' compensation doctor. A lot of people will select their primary care physician. I understand you may be comfortable with that doctor. When in workers' compensation, what is necessary is that you will tend someone as listed on that panel physicians if it is indeed valid.

Feel free to give us a call and let us help you find the right doctor because it's very, very important. Doctors actually run your workers' compensation case because they indicate how long you need to be out of work, the type of treatment that is recommended, whether you need a good specialized care from the referral or whether you need to return to work immediately.

Please give us a call because it is crucial that you follow through with the treatment. If you do not follow through with treatment that is recommended by workers' compensation doctors, we'll subject to your claim being denied by the insurance company. Don't let that happen to you.

Call us now. Again, my name is Andre' Ramsay and I'm the lawyer for the everyday worker.

Why Workers' Compensation?

https://www.youtube.com/watch?v=HLIGe3edwu4

I don't think you chose workers' compensation. Workers' compensation chooses you. I just fell in love with my clients. These people are just like me. They work every day and they work hard and to see what they went through simply because they're hurt, no fault to their own and the effects of the injuries on them and their families. I just think it was my calling and that's why I specifically focus on workers' compensation. I can do any area of law, but this is what I want to do. The firm does all areas of law totally. We have a lot of attorneys that do different things, but me personally, my calling, is for the injured worker.

I'm Andre' Ramsay, the lawyer for the everyday worker.

The Cochran Firm
and the Work in the Atlanta Community

https://www.youtube.com/watch?v=t_XRA81Mb8w

The Cochran Firm we do everything in the community that we can, and we don't do it for recognition, we do it just because the community needs to see it. The young kids need to see great role models, they need to see good people doing good things. We've done habitat for humanity, me personally I've done habitat for humanity, I enjoy doing that. We do things for high schools, we sponsor graduations, we'll show up at law clinics and provide free legal advice, any and everything that we can, whether it's to our individual churches or individual communities we'll do everything we can.

Atlanta Workers' Compensation Client Gets Advice

https://www.youtube.com/watch?v=ion0AofENps

I often advise my clients to trust the process. Listen to me and work with me. I can't do it without them and they can't do it without us I listen to what their needs are and I try to portray those needs across to the insurance company.

So because I listen to them so much, I always tell them to always communicate. Communication is key on both ends. A lot of clients will say that their previous attorneys didn't call them back, or they don't know what's going on, they're lost in the process, so I try to keep an open line of communication.

Let them know what's going on but it has to be both ways for it to work.

What Sets The Cochran Firm Atlanta Apart from the Rest?

https://www.youtube.com/watch?v=yh_eKIeeDw4

We're one of the best, that's just it. Everyone knows the Johnny Cochran legacy and that legacy lives on in every attorney that works for the firm. We take care of our clients because we care about the result. We care about what they need. If they need the medical treatment, then that's our priority, if they need the income benefits, then that's our priority. Our priorities change based on what is important to our client.

Catastrophic Workers Compensation Client Gets Help

https://www.youtube.com/watch?v=O3sLLPFSf_k

I had a client who worked for the Georgia Department of Corrections. He worked in one of the prisons. He suffered a horrific back injury. He was trying to break a fight between two inmates.

He was in the worker's compensation system for quite a while. In Georgia, if you're in the system for over 400 weeks, your income benefits stop unless your claim is deemed as catastrophic.

He had been with two or three different attorneys before, wasn't getting the result that he needed. He was now without medical treatment. He was now without income benefits.

He came to us and we did everything we could to help him, and I'm happy to say that we did.

And the best thing about it is, I didn't have to take him to court to do it. I simply just listened to everything he told me. I drafted a great brief highlighting the things that he had been going through. I discussed his treatment plan with his doctors. And after outlining everything to the insurance company, they accepted the case as catastrophic.

So as we sit here today, he is still getting the income benefits that he needs, that he deserves. He's getting the treatment that he needs and deserves, and that's really what was important to him.

Why Should A Client Choose
To Work With Our Firm?

https://www.youtube.com/watch?v=tT-FHlLoLyY

Because we care and we don't just say it, just to say it, if we're going to go out here and say we care about our clients then we have to care about each and every one of them. Whether their case is a million dollar case or whether it's a $500 case. The point is, the client feels like their case is a million dollar case every time. The client's case is important to them every time, so we have to care as well.

What Makes Andre' Ramsay Stand Out Among Other Attorneys?

https://www.youtube.com/watch?v=9CYYOeo17jY

It's simple, I just care. I care about my clients. One thing I always try to remember and keep in mind on every case is, "This is probably their first time that they've ever gotten injured on the job and this is the first time they've been in workers' compensation system." And to be quite honest, it's a terrible system. It's not great. So, though I've had thousands of clients, I always keep my client and keep my mind on this is their first time.

What Should You Expect When Working With a Workers' Comp Attorney?

https://www.youtube.com/watch?v=NSTpf6oVuZE

How do you view your role in the attorney-client relationship? I'm the voice of the client. I speak for them. Again, why communication is so important, they tell me what is important to them. A lot of times I tell my clients do not to speak to their insurance companies, don't speak to the adjusters, don't speak to your employer about your injury. Not so much that I'm concerned about what you may say, but I want to make sure we project the right image and say it at the right way, to get the right results.

Andre's Turning Point
as Workers' Comp Attorney

https://www.youtube.com/watch?v=WeTce1gxnME

O kay short story about me. I went to undergraduate studies at Florida State University and I actually graduated as a network administrator and I studied network administration for some years and worked for about 5 years before I decided to go to law school.

Now, the turning point for me while I was at Florida State University, I was selected as one of the 16 attendees for a summer law program, very prestigious program where they only select 16 students from 23 states. I was a young guy, 17 years old, didn't really know what I wanted to do, but I fell in love with the law.

Now, just like my clients who go through things in their everyday life, I went through things in undergraduate studies and I had a son and I had to provide for my son, so I started working. I was out there in the workforce.

Now, what changed for me was I received a phone call from Florida State University asking me if I ever did attend law school. My answer was no, but I thought about it, I said, well, why not? I took care of my family, I took care of my responsibilities and this is something that I want. Law is my passion, point blank simple, and I'm lucky to say that I'm able to live my dream everyday.

Frequently Asked Questions:

What is workers' compensation?

Workers' Compensation, sometimes called workers' compensation or workman's compensation, is an accident insurance program. Your employer pays for this coverage at no cost to you. If you are injured on the job, workers' compensation provides money and medical care to you. It also provides accidental death benefits to your dependents if you die as a result of a work-related injury.

Am I eligible for benefits under workers' compensation?

If you were injured on the job, yes.

How long do I have to work to be covered?

Any company employing three or more people must have workers' compensation. This includes part-time workers. You are covered the moment you start working. Workers' comp does not have the same delay as health insurance. Your employer is required, by law, to provide this insurance coverage immediately. You can verify workers' comp insurance by visiting the Verify Workers' Compensation Coverage web page.

When do I have to report an injury?

As soon as you can. The law allows you 30 days to report the injury. You must report it to your boss, foreman or supervisor. The sooner you report the injury, the better it is. If you wait more than 30 days, you could lose your benefits.

Do I have to see a doctor?

As the top workers' compensation attorneys in Atlanta, we highly recommend you see a doctor. Do not worry about medical bills. Workers' compensation pays for all your medical care, including x-rays, follow-up appointments and any necessary prescriptions.

You must see a doctor as listed on the Workers' Compensation sheet where you work, unless it is an emergency.

What if it is an emergency?

Go to the nearest emergency care facility. Do not try to make an appointment or call one of the approved doctors.

Why can't I use my doctor?

State law says you must use a doctor approved by your employer.

The list of approved doctors must be at least six physicians. You can pick from the list. In special cases, the State Workers' Compensation Board can approve less than six doctors. This is done case by case. Your employer has to ask for the waiver.

The list of doctors has to include at least one orthopedic doctor and no more than two "industrial" clinics. If possible, a minority physician must be included.

You can change from one doctor to another on the list, one time, without permission of your employer.

An employer can post a Workers' Compensation Managed Care Organization (WC/MCO) list instead of six doctors. Your employer has to tell you about this list and give you a 24-hour toll-free number to a managed care organization. If you need medical care, call that number. Someone will help you make an appointment.

Again, if it is an emergency, go to the nearest emergency care center or emergency room. Workers' compensation will take care of these bills.

What if I need a specialist?

The first doctor you see will make that determination. Again, workers' compensation will cover these bills.

Who pays for the medical care?

Workers' compensation insurance covers the bills. It covers you even if you go to an emergency room that is not listed on the sheet. The most important thing is to get the medical care you need.

What is covered?

Any authorized doctor's bill, hospital bill, physical therapy, prescriptions and necessary travel if your injury was caused by an accident on the job. You may also qualify for vocational rehabilitation. If you are injured badly enough to go to an emergency room, this is also covered.

How long can I get benefits?

In Georgia, if your injury was before June 30, 2013, you can get lifetime medical benefits. Accidents after July 1, 2013, are covered for 400 weeks after the accident date. If the injury is catastrophic, you may be entitled to lifetime benefits?

What is a catastrophic injury?

The State Board of Workers' Compensation defines a catastrophic injury as, "those involving amputations, severe paralysis, severe head injuries, severe burns, blindness, or of a nature and severity that prevents the employee from being able to perform his or her prior work and any work available in substantial numbers within the national economy. In catastrophic cases, you are entitled to receive two-thirds of your average weekly wage up to the maximum allowed under the law for a job-related injury for as long as you are unable to return to work."

When do my benefits start?

You can receive benefits if you are out of work for seven days. You should get a check within 21 days after the first day of missed work. If you miss more than 21 days in a row, you will also get a check for the first week you could not work.

How much will I get?

You can get two-thirds of your average weekly pay, but not more than $550 a week for any accident that happened on or after July 1, 2015.

If you can go back to work part-time or reduced hours or for less pay, you can continue to get reduced benefits for up to 350 weeks. In this case, you can't get more than $367 a week if your accident happened on or after July 1, 2015.

How long can I get benefits?

Up to 400 weeks. If your injury is catastrophic, you can have benefits for life.

What if my injury keeps me from getting a job?

You can get help to learn how to do another job. If you can't work at all, you may be entitled to lifetime help. The Cochran Firm, (404) 724-8181, can tell you more about this. The State Board of Workers' Compensation, (404) 656-0849, also has more information.

What benefits will I get if my injury causes permanent disability?

This depends on the injury. The doctor handling your medical care will decide, using the Guides to the Evaluation of Permanent Impairment fifth edition, published by the American Medical Association. If you think you are not being treated fairly, contact us immediately. You can appeal the physician's decision.

What if I lose an arm, a leg or some other body part?

State law determines how much you can receive. We can tell you if you are being treated fairly if this happens to you.

What if I am blinded or made deaf?

You qualify for benefits. We can also tell you if you are receiving a fair settlement.

What if I lose the ability to use part of my body?

You can get benefits. The doctor will decide how much the loss affects you. Sometimes a doctor's evaluation doesn't cover your actual losses. We'll be glad to review your case for you.

What are death benefits?

When an employee is killed on the job, state law allows surviving dependents to collect two-thirds of your weekly pay up to $550 a week. Dependents are your spouse, minor children and step-children. A surviving spouse with no children is allowed up to $220,000. in total money benefits.

Can I get Workers' Compensation and Social Security at the same time?

Yes. Your Social Security may be reduced.

What if I am not getting my workers' compensation benefits?

Contact The Cochran Firm immediately at (404) 724-8181. You have a year after the injury to file for benefits. You should also file a Form WC-14 with the State Board of Workers' Compensation.

How do I file a claim?

Your employer should start the process for you. You will have to fill out some forms. If you can't, someone will help you. If you can't sign the forms, others will have to witness this for you. The State Board of Workers' Compensation will give you a Form WC-14. You can also call the Board at (404) 656-3818 in Atlanta and 1-800-533-0682 outside the metro Atlanta area.

What happens when I file a claim?

You should start getting benefits. If you do not get benefits, call The

Cochran Firm immediately at (404) 724-8181. If you think you are not being treated fairly or are being denied benefits, call us.

We'll review your claim. We may decide that you need to have a hearing. If you need to go to a hearing, we will represent you and advise you every step of the way. We'll tell you when the hearing is and where it will be. It's usually held within 60 days of the request for a hearing and near where you work.

Do I need a lawyer?

The law says you do not. But you could be facing lawyers for your employer and the insurance company. The Cochran Firm's attorneys know the Georgia workers' compensation law. We will represent you and make sure all your rights are protected.

How much will a lawyer cost me?

The State Board of Workers' Compensation approves any fee of more than $100. It cannot be more than 25 percent of your financial award. We will explain the fee to you and make sure you thoroughly understand it before you sign.

Conclusion

It is our hope that this guide will help educate injured workers' about their rights, and answer questions about workers' compensation. If you are facing a legal issue and need help, please contact me directly at aramsay@cochranfirmatl.com or call our firm directly at 404-222-9922. There is no fee or obligation for the first consultation.

You can also visit our website http://workerscompensationanswers.com. As an attorney, I knew that it was important to create a website that provides our current and prospective clients with educational and informative content. Our site features an entire section dedicated to videos that we have recorded that answer questions about Workers' Compensation.

Each page on the website explains more about our practice area of the law and what Cochran Firm Atlanta – Workers' Compensation does. We have made the experience more engaging by creating a variety of ways for you to interact with the site and to access the information you want.

About the Author:

Attorney Andre' C. Ramsay joined The Cochran Firm Atlanta in 2016. He previously worked as an Associate Attorney at a fast-paced North Atlanta law firm specializing in the practice areas of Workers' Compensation, Personal Injury, and Social Security Disability. Mr. Ramsay aggressively represents many injured workers in acquiring all income and medical benefits available to them to the full extent of the law.

Andre' earned a bachelor's degree in Management of Information

Studies, with a minor in Business Administration from Florida State University. As an undergraduate student, Andre' was one of 16 students chosen from 23 states for the Florida State University College of Law National Summer Law Program.

Andre' later earned his Juris Doctorate degree from Atlanta's John Marshall Law School. While in law school, Andre' competed in the American Bar Association Client Interviewing and Counseling competition where he placed in the "National Top-6" after winning the Regional competition. Andre' also founded the Caribbean Law Students Association, was a Student Bar Association Class Representative, and a Pre-Trial CALI award recipient. Andre' also clerked for a well-known national law firm, where he had the opportunity to work directly under a former Georgia Workers' Compensation Administrative Law Judge.

www.ingramcontent.com/pod-product-compliance
Lightning Source LLC
Chambersburg PA
CBHW060624210326
41520CB00010B/1463